FLUTE/OBOE

ENSEMBLE DEVELOPMENT

Chorales and Warm-up Exercises for Tone, Technique and Rhythm

YOUNG CONCERT BAND

Peter **BOONSHAFT** | Chris **BERNOTAS**

Thank you for making *Sound Innovations Ensemble Development for Young Concert Band* a part of your large ensemble curriculum. With 167 exercises, including more than 100 chorales by some of today's most renowned young band composers, this book will be a valuable resource in helping you grow in your understanding and abilities as an ensemble musician.

An assortment of exercises, grouped by key, are presented in a variety of young band difficulty levels. Where possible, several exercises in the same category are provided to allow variety while accomplishing the goals of that specific type of exercise. You will notice that many exercises and chorales are clearly marked with dynamics, articulations, style and tempo for you to practice those aspects of performance. Other exercises are intentionally left for you or your teacher to determine how best to use them in reaching your performance goals.

Whether you are progressing through exercises to better your technical facility or challenging your musicianship with beautiful chorales, we are confident you will be excited, motivated and inspired by using *Sound Innovations Ensemble Development for Young Concert Band.*

ISBN-10: 1-4706-3387-6
ISBN-13: 978-1-4706-3387-5

Instrument photos courtesy of Yamaha Corporation of America Band & Orchestral Division

Concert B♭ Major

1 **LONG TONES**

2 **PASSING THE TONIC**

3 **PASSING THE TONIC**

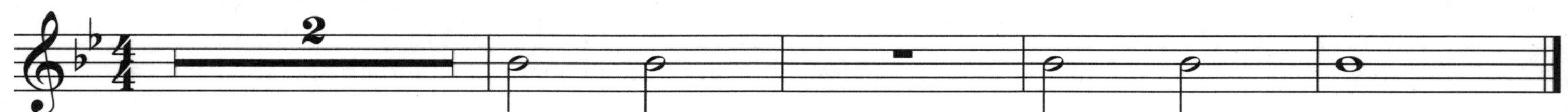

4 **PITCH MATCHING: WOODWIND MOUTHPIECES WITH BAND ACCOMPANIMENT**

** Match the pitch on the headjoint alone.*
+ Oboe should play on the instrument as usual.

5 **SCALE BUILDER**

6 **SCALE BUILDER**

7 EXPANDING INTERVALS: DIATONIC

8 EXPANDING INTERVALS: CHROMATIC

9 INTERVAL BUILDER: DIATONIC INTERVALS

10 INTERVAL BUILDER: PERFECT INTERVALS

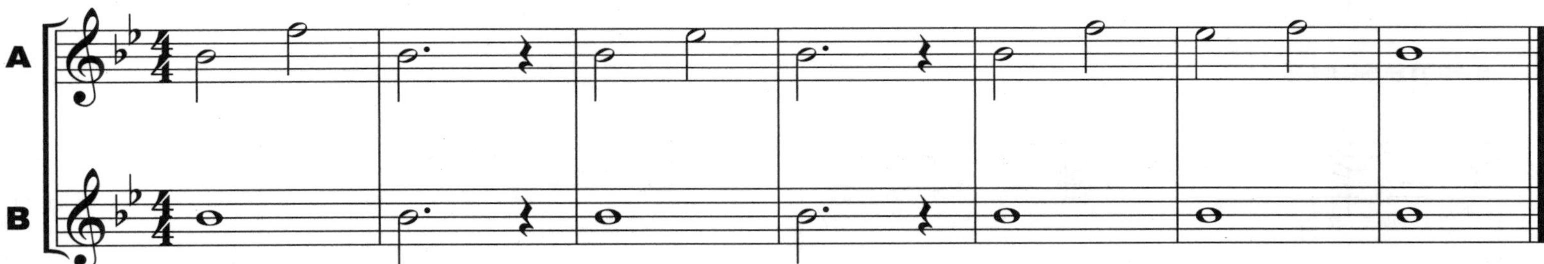

11 CHORD BUILDER

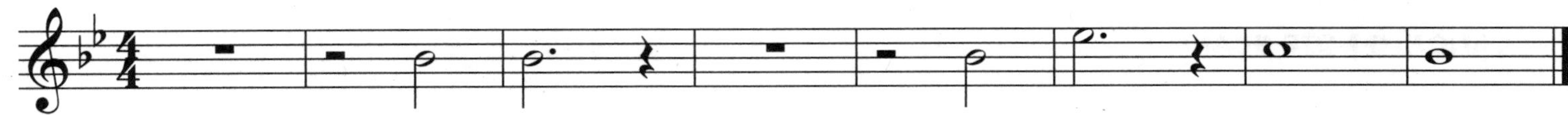

12 CHORD BUILDER

13 MOVING CHORD TONES

14 DIATONIC HARMONY

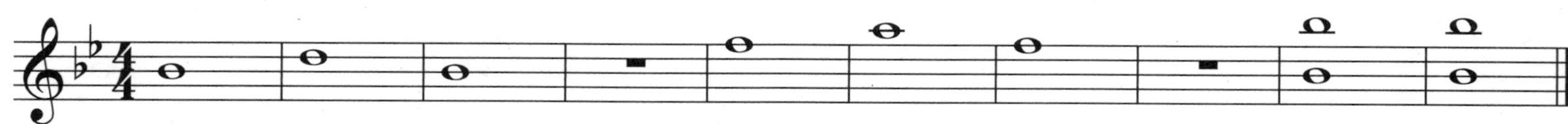

15 DIATONIC HARMONY

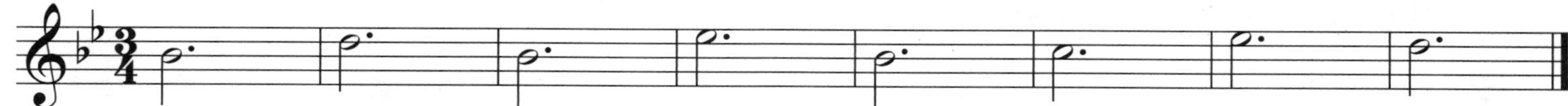

16 RHYTHMIC SOUNDS

Play the repeated section at least 4 times.

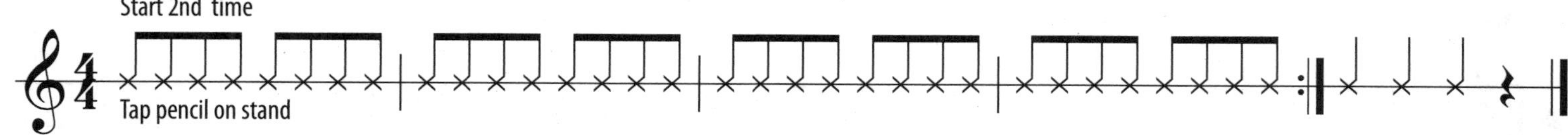

17 RHYTHMIC SUBDIVISION

18 5-NOTE SCALE

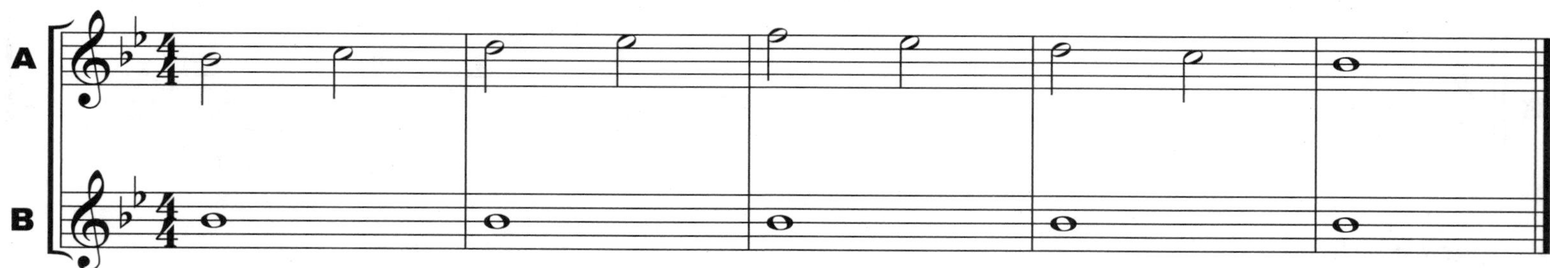

19 CANON: 5-NOTE SCALE

20 CANON: 6-NOTE SCALE

21 CANON: 8-NOTE SCALE

22 **CHORALE: 5-NOTE SCALE**

Chris M. Bernotas (ASCAP)

23 **CHORALE: 5-NOTE SCALE**

Chris M. Bernotas (ASCAP)

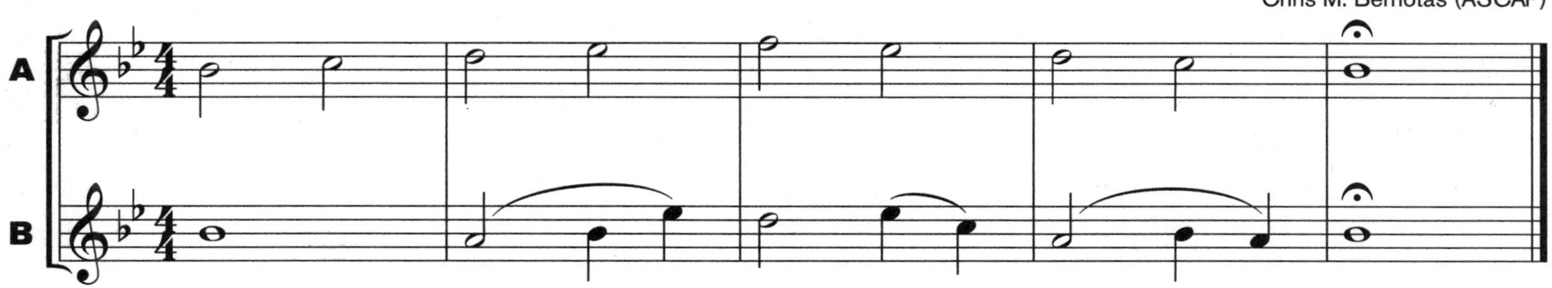

24 **CHORALE: 6-NOTE SCALE**

Chris M. Bernotas (ASCAP)

25 **CHORALE: 8-NOTE SCALE**

Chris M. Bernotas (ASCAP)

26 **CHORALE: 8-NOTE SCALE**

Chris M. Bernotas (ASCAP)

27 CHORALE

Robert Sheldon (ASCAP)

28 CHORALE

John O'Reilly (ASCAP)

29 CHORALE

Ralph Ford (ASCAP)

30 CHORALE

Michael Story (ASCAP)

31 CHORALE

Randall D. Standridge (ASCAP)

32 CHORALE

Roland Barrett (ASCAP)

33 CHORALE

Chris M. Bernotas (ASCAP)

34 CHORALE

Rob Grice (ASCAP)

35 CHORALE
Very smoothly
Matt Conaway (ASCAP)
mf
36 CHORALE
Largo
Scott Watson (BMI)
mf
f
rit.
37 CHORALE
Todd Stalter (ASCAP)
Maestoso
mf
38 CHORALE
Robert Sheldon (ASCAP)
mf
39 CHORALE
Tyler S. Grant (ASCAP)
Moderately
mp
mf
f
p rit.
40 CHORALE
Randall D. Standridge (ASCAP)
1
mf
f
2
mf
f
41 CHORALE
Todd Stalter (ASCAP)
Maestoso
1
mf
2
mf
42 CHORALE
Michael Story (ASCAP)
Moderately slow
mf

43
CHORALE
Ralph Ford (ASCAP)
mf
f
44
CHORALE
Andante
John O'Reilly (ASCAP)
mp
45
CHORALE
"Finally the first smells of Summer were in the air. 'Time to plant those strange seeds we found,' she thought."
Jodie Blackshaw (ASCAP)
mp
mp
mf
mp
46
CHORALE
Gently flowing
Matt Conaway (ASCAP)
1
2
mp
mp
47
CHORALE
Randall D. Standridge (ASCAP)
mf
f
48
CHORALE
Robert Sheldon (ASCAP)
1
2
49
CHORALE
Slowly
Chris M. Bernotas (ASCAP)
mp
mf
mp
mf
50
CHORALE
Roland Barrett (ASCAP)
mf

Concert G Minor

51 **LONG TONES**

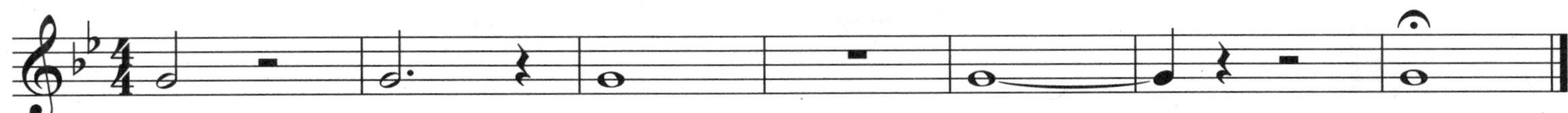

52 **PASSING THE TONIC**

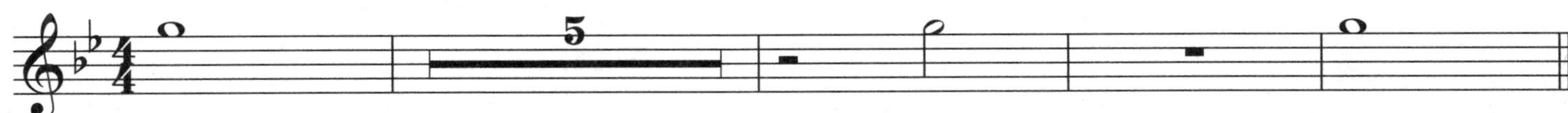

53 **EXPANDING INTERVALS: DIATONIC**

54 **INTERVAL BUILDER: DIATONIC INTERVALS**

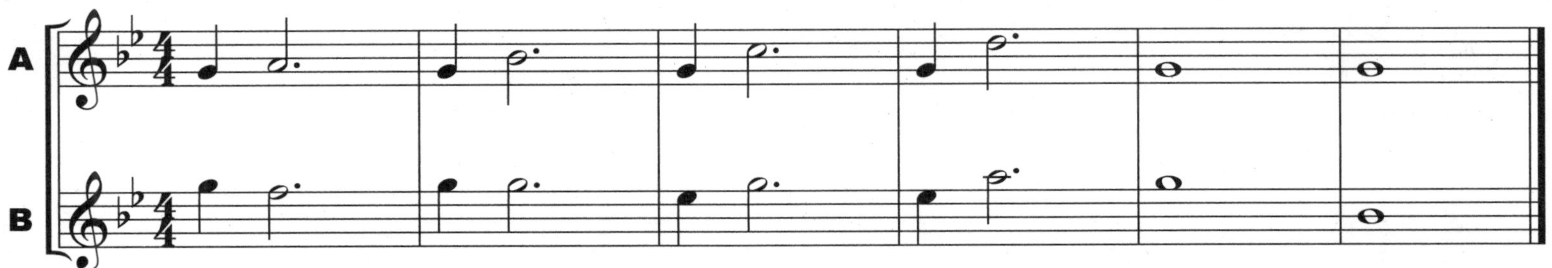

55 **CHORD BUILDER**

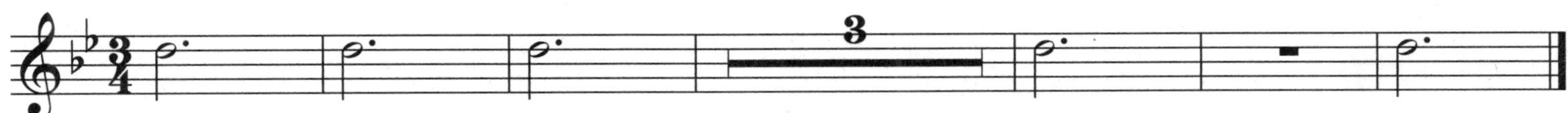

56 **DIATONIC HARMONY**

57 **CHORALE: 5-NOTE SCALE**

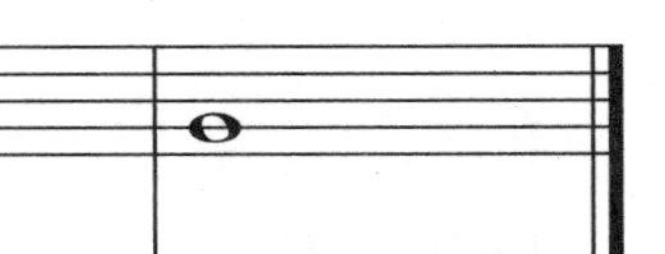

58 CHORALE: 8-NOTE SCALE (NATURAL MINOR)

Chris M. Bernotas (ASCAP)

59 CHORALE: 8-NOTE SCALE (HARMONIC MINOR)

Chris M. Bernotas (ASCAP)

60 CHORALE

Tyler S. Grant (ASCAP)

61 CHORALE

Rob Grice (ASCAP)

62 CHORALE

Robert Sheldon (ASCAP)

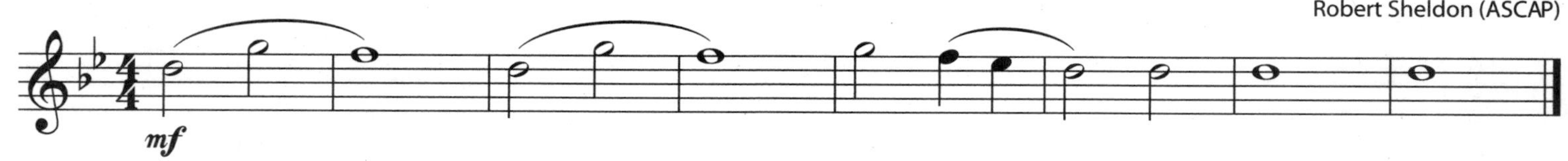

63 CHORALE

Michael Story (ASCAP)

64 CHORALE

Randall D. Standridge (ASCAP)

1

mp mf mp f

2

mp mf mp f

65 CHORALE
Scott Watson (BMI)
Lento
mp
molto rit.
f
66 CHORALE
Matt Conaway (ASCAP)
p
mf
mp
67 CHORALE
Roland Barrett (ASCAP)
mf
p
68 CHORALE
John O'Reilly (ASCAP)
Adagio
mp
69 CHORALE
Chris M. Bernotas (ASCAP)
Slowly
1
2
mp
mf
70 CHORALE
Ralph Ford (ASCAP)
p
mf
p
71 CHORALE
Tyler S. Grant (ASCAP)
Andante
mp
mf
p
72 CHORALE
"She was determined to seek the truth, even if it meant losing everything."
Jodie Blackshaw (ASCAP)
mf
f
mp

Concert E♭ Major

73 **LONG TONES**

74 **LONG TONES**

75 **PASSING THE TONIC**

76 **PASSING THE TONIC**

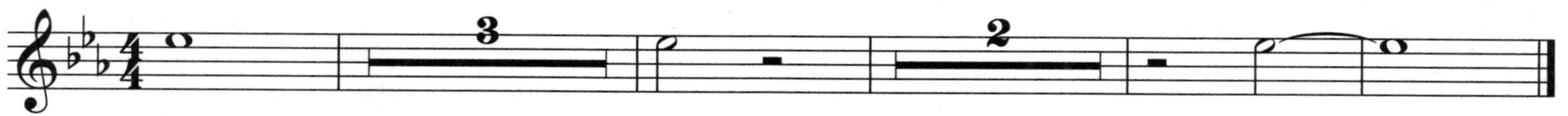

77 **SCALE BUILDER**

78 **SCALE BUILDER**

79 **EXPANDING INTERVALS: DIATONIC**

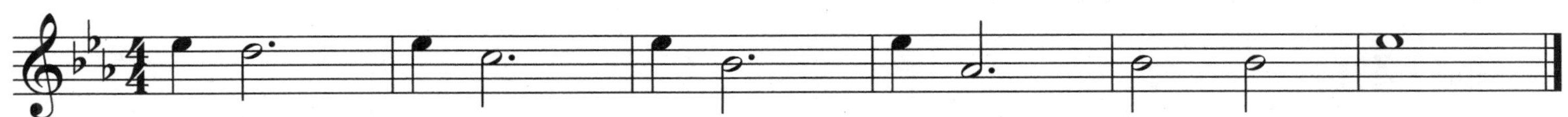

80 **EXPANDING INTERVALS: CHROMATIC**

81 **INTERVAL BUILDER: DIATONIC INTERVALS**

82 **INTERVAL BUILDER: PERFECT INTERVALS**

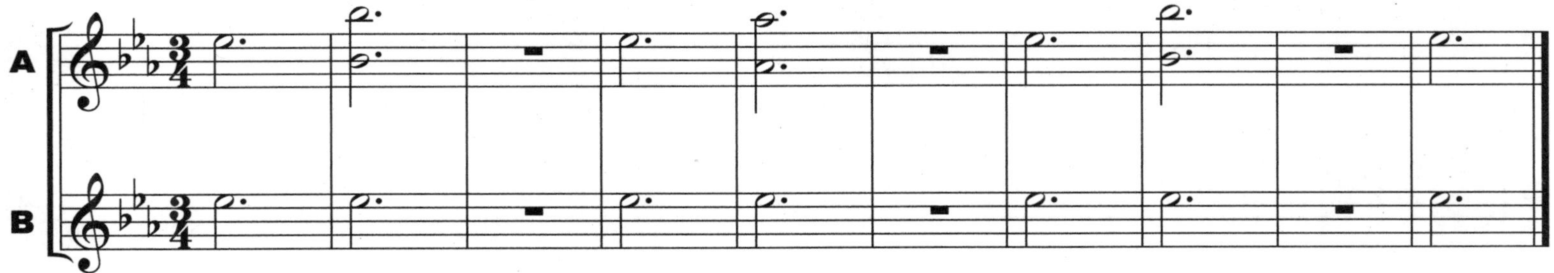

83 **CHORD BUILDER**

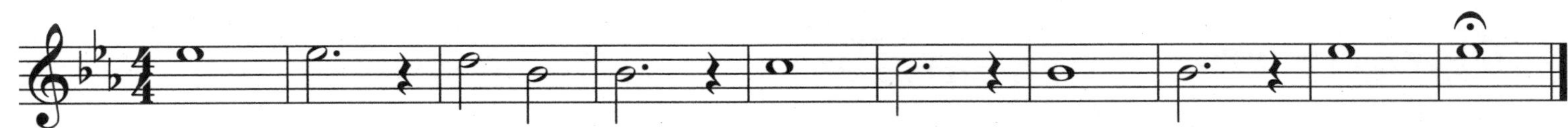

84 **CHORD BUILDER**

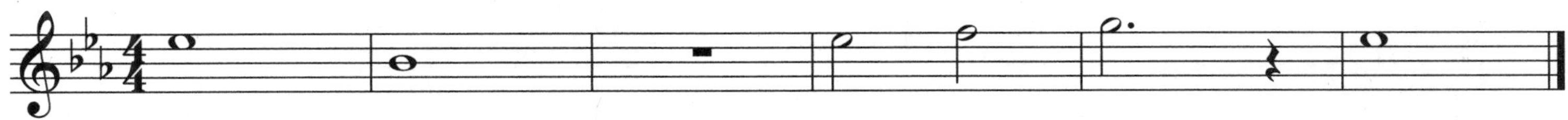

85 **MOVING CHORD TONES**

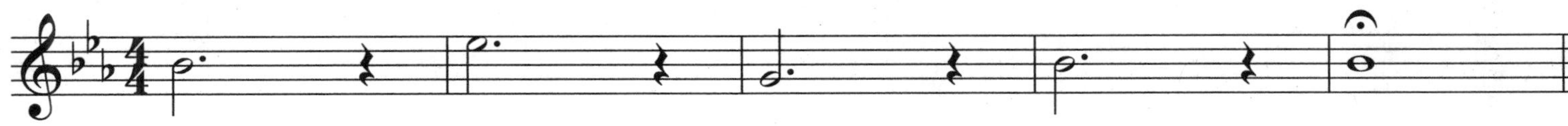

86 **DIATONIC HARMONY**

87 **DIATONIC HARMONY**

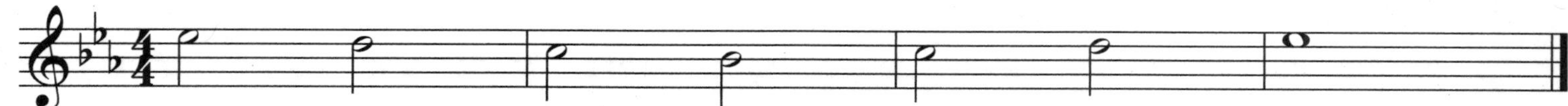

88 **RHYTHMIC SUBDIVISION**

89 **5-NOTE SCALE**

90 **CANON: 5-NOTE SCALE**

91 **CANON: 6-NOTE SCALE**

92 **CANON: 8-NOTE SCALE**

93 CHORALE: 5-NOTE SCALE
Chris M. Bernotas (ASCAP)
A
B
94 CHORALE: 5-NOTE SCALE
Chris M. Bernotas (ASCAP)
A
B
95 CHORALE: 6-NOTE SCALE
Chris M. Bernotas (ASCAP)
A
B
96 CHORALE: 8-NOTE SCALE
Chris M. Bernotas (ASCAP)
A
B
97 CHORALE: 8-NOTE SCALE
Chris M. Bernotas (ASCAP)
A
B

98 CHORALE

Todd Stalter (ASCAP)

Maestoso

99 CHORALE

Michael Story (ASCAP)

Moderately slow

100 CHORALE

Rob Grice (ASCAP)

101 CHORALE

Matt Conaway (ASCAP)

Gently

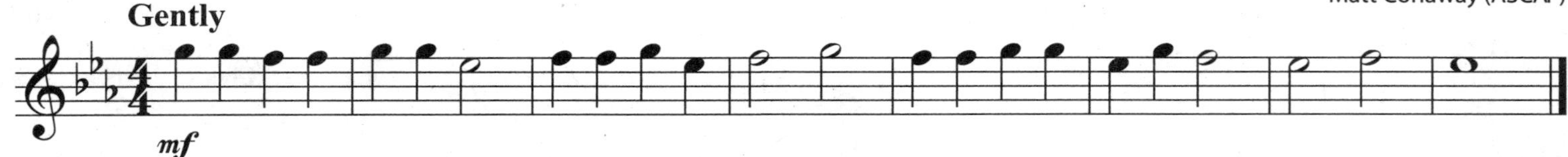

102 CHORALE

John O'Reilly (ASCAP)

Moderato

103 CHORALE

Scott Watson (BMI)

Moderato

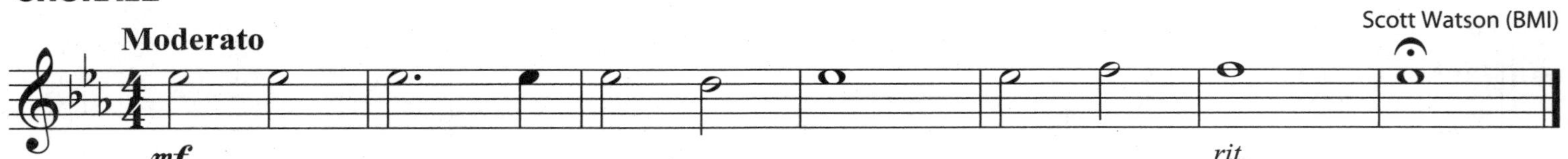

104 CHORALE

Roland Barrett (ASCAP)

105 CHORALE

Ralph Ford (ASCAP)

Espressivo

106 CHORALE
Rob Grice (ASCAP)
1
2
mf
f
rit.
107 CHORALE
Tyler S. Grant (ASCAP)
Andante rubato
p
mf
p
f
p
108 CHORALE
Chris M. Bernotas (ASCAP)
Slowly
mp
mf
f
109 CHORALE
Robert Sheldon (ASCAP)
mf
110 CHORALE
Todd Stalter (ASCAP)
Maestoso
mf
111 CHORALE
Jodie Blackshaw (ASCAP)
"In the mist there lurked a dark shadowy figure. Could it be?"
mp
mf
poco rit.
mp
112 CHORALE
Matt Conaway (ASCAP)
mf
f
mp
113 CHORALE
Tyler S. Grant (ASCAP)
mp
mf

114 CHORALE

Andante

John O'Reilly (ASCAP)

mf

115 CHORALE

Moderately slow

Michael Story (ASCAP)

mf

rit.

116 CHORALE

Andante

Todd Stalter (ASCAP)

1

mf

2

mf

117 CHORALE

Randall D. Standridge (ASCAP)

mf

f

118 CHORALE

Maestoso

Scottish Psalter, 1635
Arranged by Scott Watson (BMI)

mf

rit.

119 CHORALE

"Heart pounding he opened his eyes. A dull light grew to reveal a world he had never seen before."

Jodie Blackshaw (ASCAP)

pp

mp

p

120 CHORALE

Slowly

Chris M. Bernotas (ASCAP)

mp

mf

121 CHORALE

Matt Conaway (ASCAP)

1

mp

f

2

mp

f

Concert C Minor

122 **LONG TONES**

123 **PASSING THE TONIC**

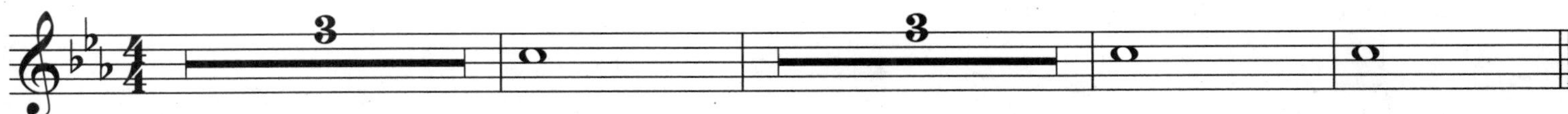

124 **EXPANDING INTERVALS: DIATONIC**

125 **INTERVAL BUILDER: DIATONIC INTERVALS**

126 **CHORD BUILDER**

127 **DIATONIC HARMONY**

128 **CHORALE: 5-NOTE SCALE**

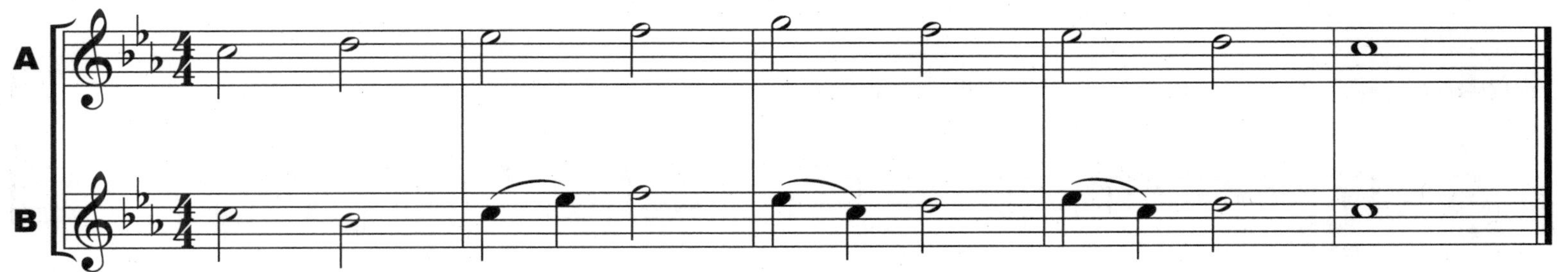

129 **CHORALE: 8-NOTE SCALE (NATURAL MINOR)**

Chris M. Bernotas (ASCAP)

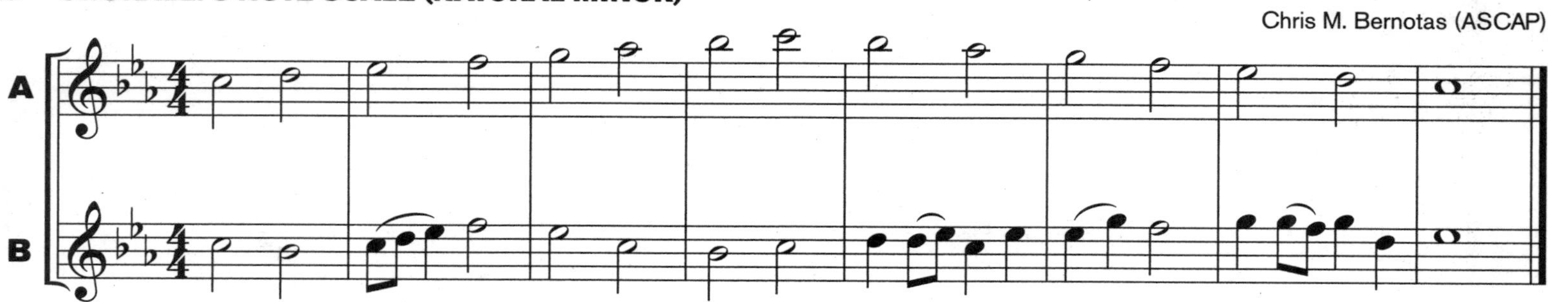

130 **CHORALE: 8-NOTE SCALE (HARMONIC MINOR)**

Chris M. Bernotas (ASCAP)

131 **CHORALE**

Tyler S. Grant (ASCAP)

132 **CHORALE**

Rob Grice (ASCAP)

133 **CHORALE**

Ralph Ford (ASCAP)

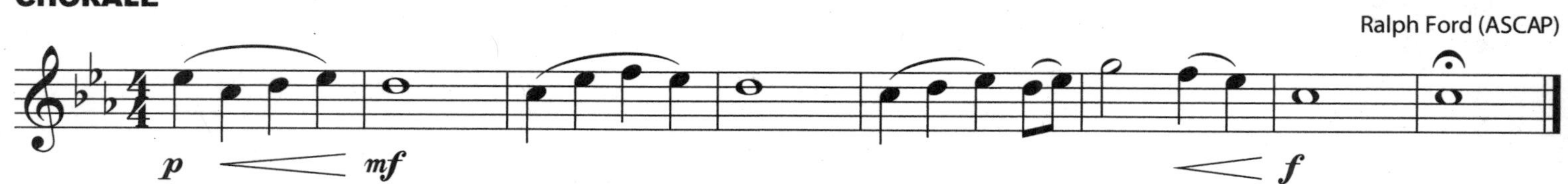

134 **CHORALE**

Robert Sheldon (ASCAP)

135 **CHORALE**

Michael Story (ASCAP)

136 CHORALE
Scott Watson (BMI)
1
2
p
mp
p
molto rit.
mf
137 CHORALE
Matt Conaway (ASCAP)
mf
p
138 CHORALE
Rob Grice (ASCAP)
mf
f
139 CHORALE
Chris M. Bernotas (ASCAP)
Largo
f
140 CHORALE
Randall D. Standridge (ASCAP)
mf
141 CHORALE
"Through the haze they glared at each other. He'd been waiting a long time for this."
Jodie Blackshaw (ASCAP)
mp
mf
142 CHORALE
Roland Barrett (ASCAP)
mf
mp
143 CHORALE
John O'Reilly (ASCAP)
Adagio
mf

Concert F Major

144 **PASSING THE TONIC**

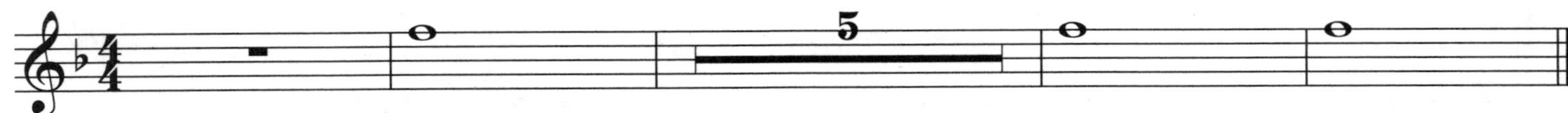

145 **EXPANDING INTERVALS: CHROMATIC**

146 **CHORD BUILDER**

147 **DIATONIC HARMONY**

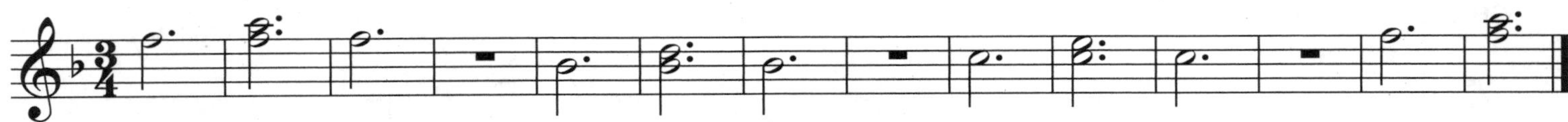

148 **CHORALE: 6-NOTE SCALE**

Chris M. Bernotas (ASCAP)

149 **CHORALE**

Rob Grice (ASCAP)

150 **CHORALE**

Ralph Ford (ASCAP)

151 **CHORALE**

Scott Watson (BMI)

152 CHORALE
Randall D. Standridge (ASCAP)
mf
153 CHORALE
Andante
John O'Reilly (ASCAP)
mf
154 CHORALE
Roland Barrett (ASCAP)
mf
mp
155 CHORALE
Adapted from Psalm 150, Claude Goudimel
Arranged by Todd Stalter (ASCAP)
Maestoso
mf
Concert D Minor
156 PASSING THE TONIC
3
157 CHORD BUILDER
158 DIATONIC HARMONY
159 CHORALE: 8-NOTE SCALE (HARMONIC MINOR)
Chris M. Bernotas (ASCAP)
A
B

160 CHORALE

Roland Barrett (ASCAP)

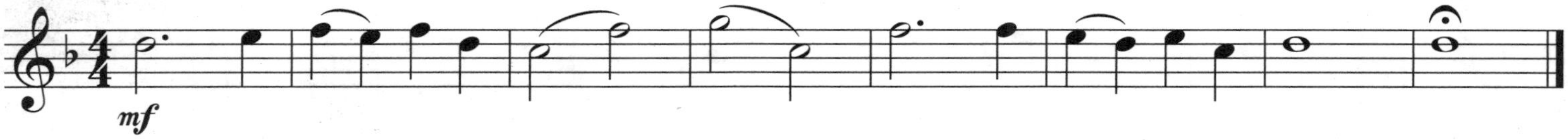

mf

161 CHORALE

Robert Sheldon (ASCAP)

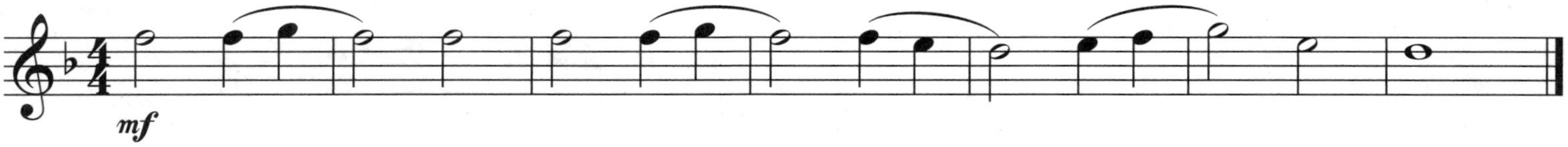

mf

162 CHORALE

Todd Stalter (ASCAP)

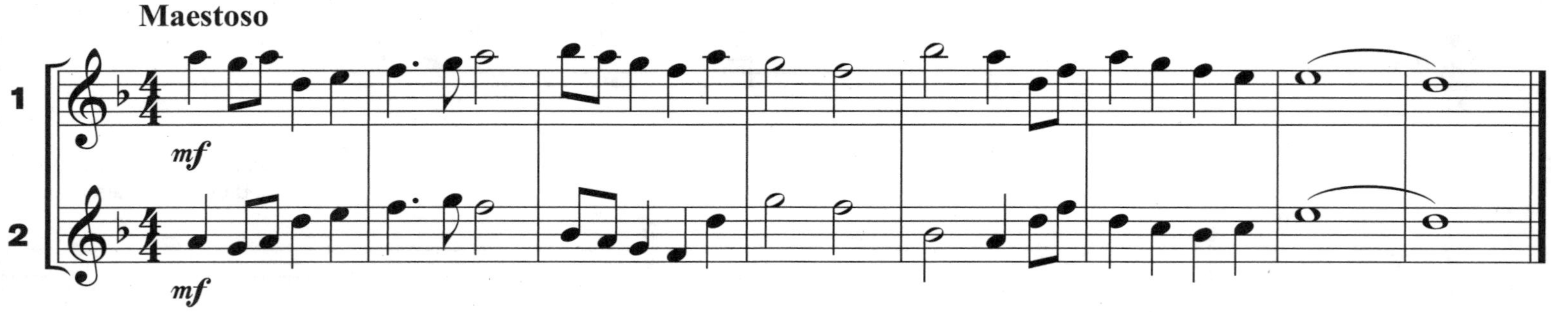

Maestoso
1
2
mf
mf

163 CHORALE

Scott Watson (BMI)

Adagio
mf
rit.

164 CHORALE

Michael Story (ASCAP)

Moderately slow
mf

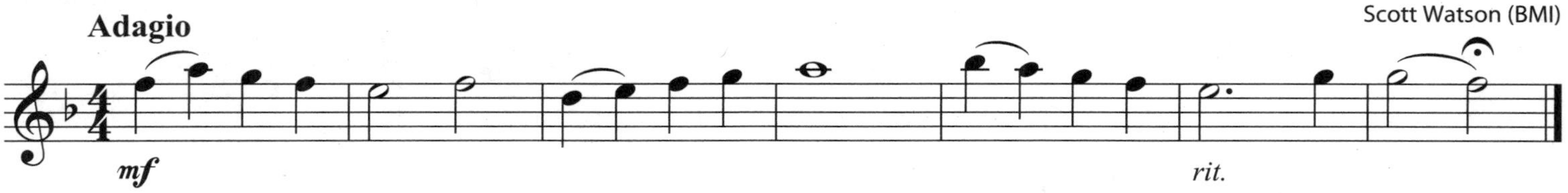

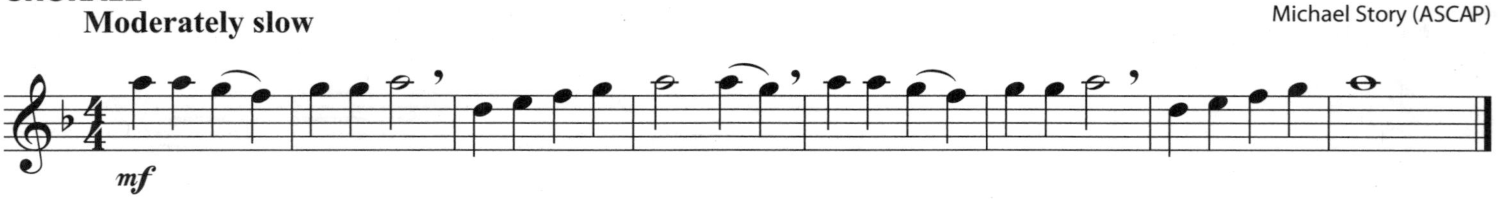

165 CHORALE

Ralph Ford (ASCAP)

p
mf
f
pp

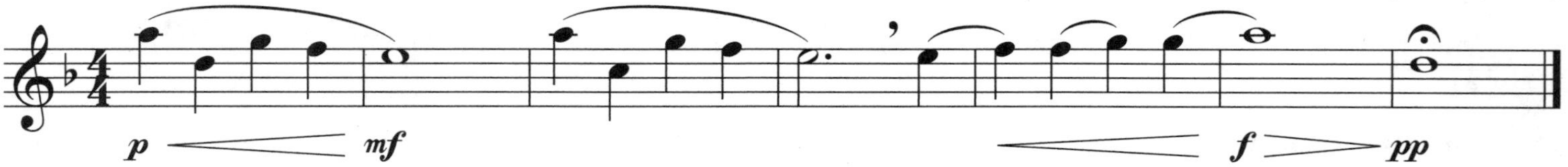

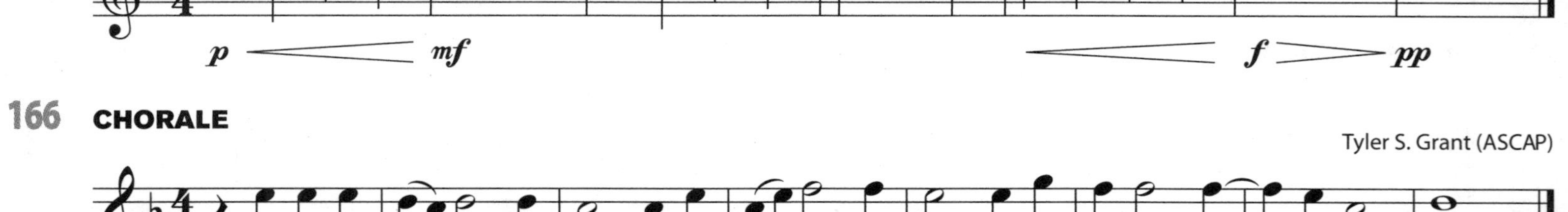

166 CHORALE

Tyler S. Grant (ASCAP)

p
mf

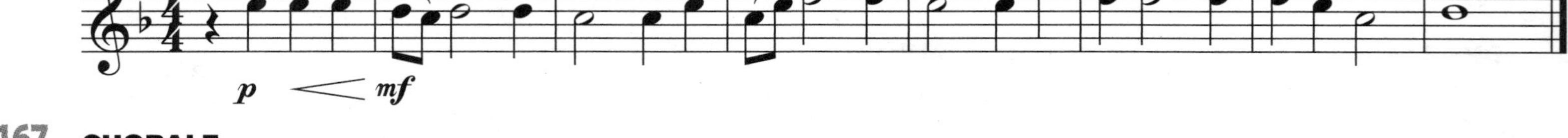

167 CHORALE

"In the darkness all she could hear was the sound of her beating heart. What had she done?"

Jodie Blackshaw (ASCAP)

mf
f
mf

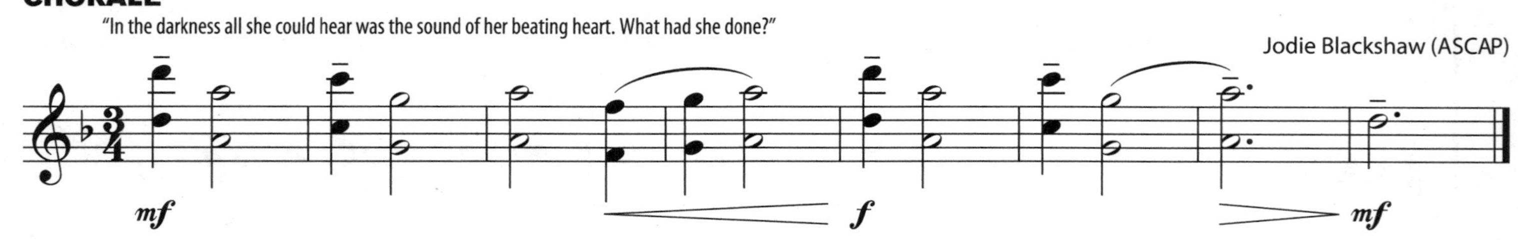